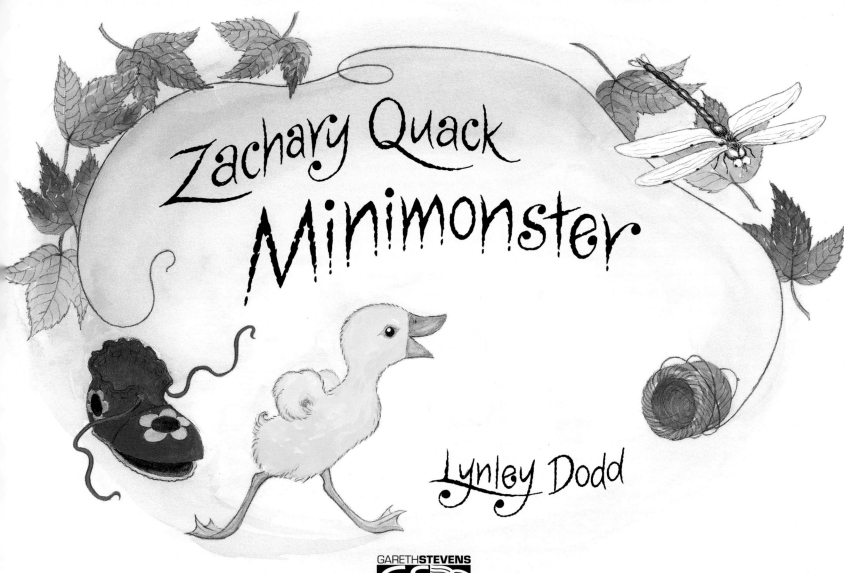

Zachary Quack
Minimonster

Lynley Dodd

GARETH**STEVENS**

GS

PUBLISHING

A Member of the WRC Media Family of Companies

Climbing the riverbank
onto the track,
went pittery pattery
Zachary Quack.

3

He scruffled a centipede
out of its house,
he pestered a spider
and ruffled a mouse.

He bustled a beetle
asleep on a chair,
and hustled a dragonfly
into the air.

FLICK
went the dragonfly,
FLICK FLICK FLICK,
here, there, and everywhere,
quick,
quick,
quick.

Over the path
and the rockery too,

over some paint
and a bottle of glue.

FLICK
went the dragonfly,
FLICK FLICK FLICK,
here, there, and everywhere,
quick,
quick,
quick.

Through the petunias,
pumpkins, and peas,

over the rake
and a mountain of leaves.

FLICK
went the dragonfly,
FLICK FLICK FLICK,
here, there, and everywhere,
quick,
quick,
quick.

Over the sandbox,
around the old swing,

the netting and potting mix,
tied up with string.

FLICK
went the dragonfly,
FLICK FLICK FLICK,

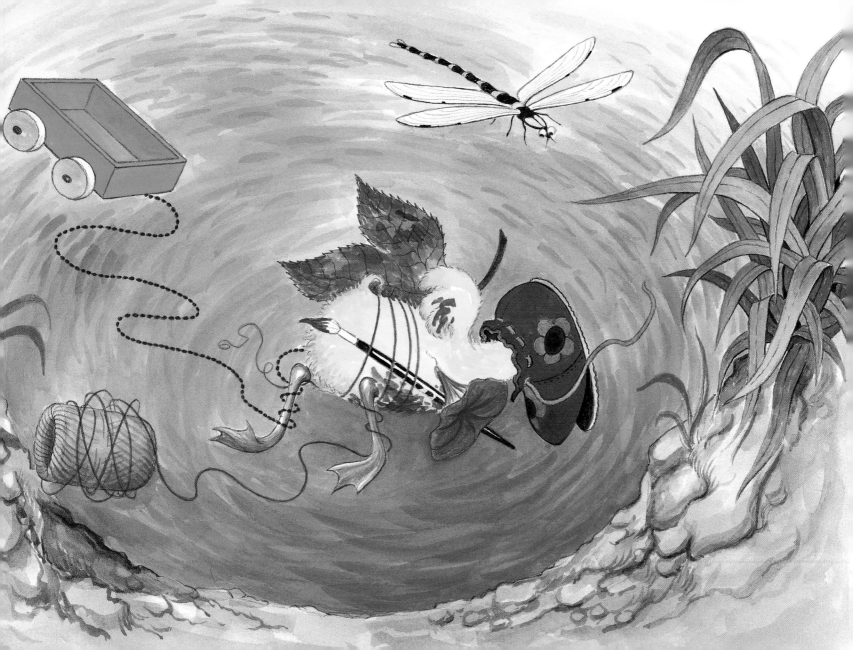

back to the riverbank,
quick,
quick,

QUICK!

Please visit our web site at: www.garethstevens.com
For a free color catalog describing Gareth Stevens Publishing's list of high-quality
books and multimedia programs, call 1-800-542-2595 (USA) or 1-800-387-3178 (Canada).
Gareth Stevens Publishing's fax: (414) 332-3567.

Other GOLD STAR FIRST READER
Millennium Editions:

A Dragon in a Wagon
Find Me a Tiger
Hairy Maclary from Donaldson's Dairy
Hairy Maclary Scattercat
Hairy Maclary, Sit
Hairy Maclary and Zachary Quack
Hairy Maclary's Bone
Hairy Maclary's Caterwaul Caper
Hairy Maclary's Rumpus at the Vet
Hairy Maclary's Showbusiness
Hedgehog Howdedo
Scarface Claw
Schnitzel von Krumm, Dogs Never Climb Trees
Schnitzel von Krumm Forget-Me-Not

Schnitzel von Krumm's Basketwork
Slinky Malinki
Slinky Malinki, Open the Door
The Smallest Turtle
SNIFF-SNUFF-SNAP!
Wake Up, Bear

and also by Lynley Dodd:
The Minister's Cat ABC
Slinky Malinki Catflaps

Library of Congress Cataloging-in-Publication Data

Dodd, Lynley.
    Zachary Quack minimonster / Lynley Dodd.
        p. cm. — (Gold star first readers)
    Summary: A duckling follows a dragonfly and accidentally changes into a small monster.
    ISBN 0-8368-6187-6 (lib. bdg.)
    [1. Ducks—Fiction. 2. Dragonflies—Fiction. 3. Monsters—Fiction. 4. Stories in rhyme.]
    I. Title: Zachary Quack minimonster. II. Series.
    PZ8.3.D637Zac   2006
    [E]—dc22   2005044483

This edition first published in 2006 by
Gareth Stevens Publishing
A Member of the WRC Media Family of Companies
330 West Olive Street, Suite 100
Milwaukee, WI 53212 USA

First published in 2005 in New Zealand by Mallinson Rendel Publishers Ltd. Original © 2005 by Lynley Dodd.

Printed in the United States of America

1 2 3 4 5 6 7 8 9 10 09 08 07 06